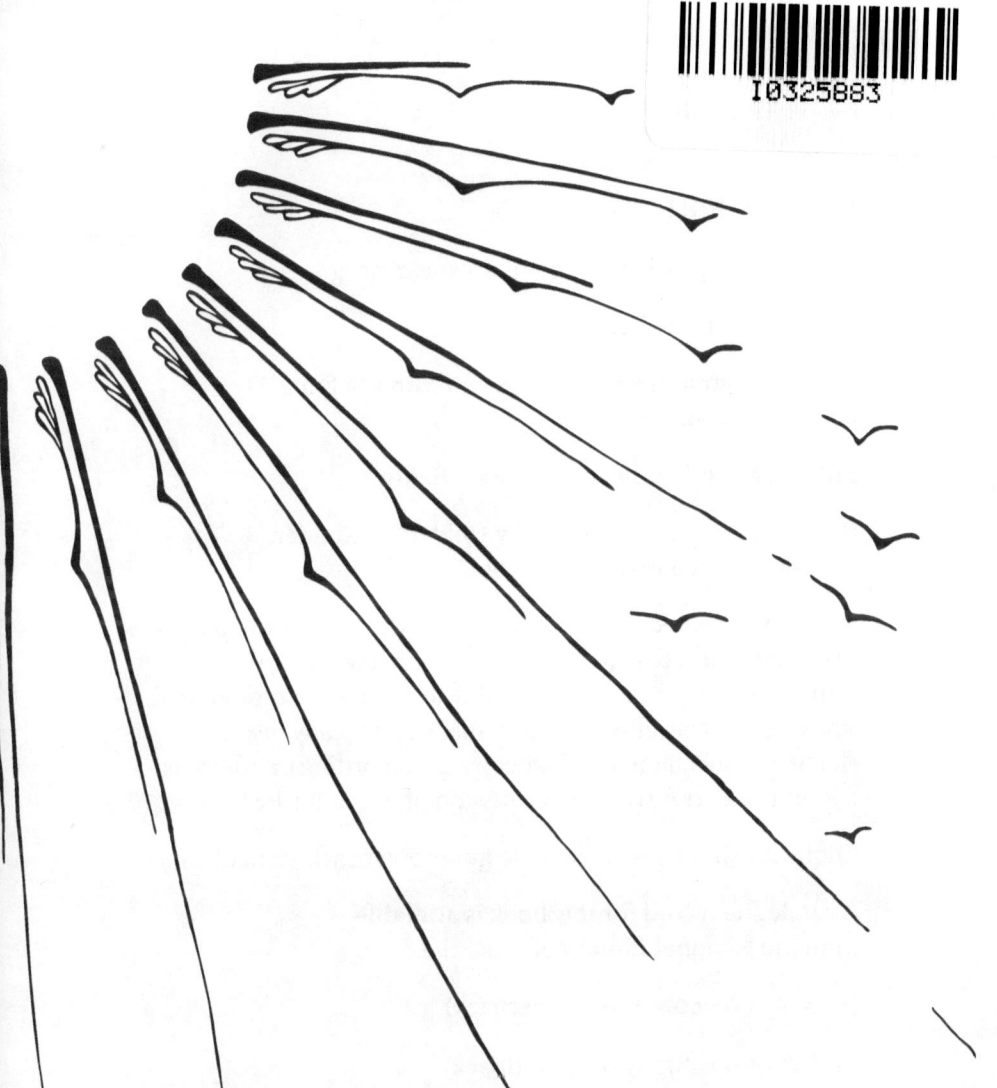

ILLUMINATIONS
19 Poems and 1 Story

First Published in Australia 2020

© Gumbootspearlz Press gumbootspearlz.org

© 2020 Text June Perkins

© 2020 Illustrations Ruha Fifita and Minaira Fifita
ivi-designs.com

Editors: Matilda Elliot and Belinda Belton

Book format and typesetting by Heidi Den Ronden
heididenronden.myportfolio.com

All rights reserved. Apart from any fair dealing for the purposes of private study, research, criticism or review under the Copyright Act, no part of this publication may be reproduced, stored in a retrieval system, or transmitted by any means electronic, mechanical, photocopying, recording or otherwise without the prior written permission of the publisher.

Enquiries should be emailed to gumbootspearlz@gmail.com

A catalogue record for this book is available
from the National Library of Australia.

ISBN: 978-0-9807311-9-4 (Paperback)

ISBN: 978-0-6487205-0-8 (Hardback)

Dedication

This work honours the Bicentenary of the Birth of the Báb and the Bicentenary of the Birth of Bahá'u'lláh

Contents

Acknowledgements … v
Foreword … vii
The Dreamer … 1
Artist's Riddle … 2
Boonah Morning … 5
The Poetry Bird … 6
Poet's Tree … 8
Nine Illuminations … 10
Swirling, Almost Something … 16
Declaration … 23
First Light … 25
Dawn Breakers … 26
In Faith … 30
The Green Broom … 32
Prince of Peace … 35
Dust … 40
Slipstream … 42
Elixir … 45
Word Fragrance … 46

Dear Artist	48
Hope	52
Listen	55
Notes to the Poems	56
Biographies	63
From the Readers	65

Acknowledgements

Earlier versions of poems in this collection appear in:

Tokens, issues 7-9, (2018-19) Bahá'ís of Philadelphia ed. James Tichenor

www.ripplepoetry.wordpress.com

Quotation prior to 'Declaration', Source: *Selections of the Writings of the Báb*, by the Báb
www.bahai.org/library/authoritative-texts/the-bab/selections-writings-bab/3#446094665

Quotation prior to 'Prince of Peace', Source: No 4, Persian, *The Hidden Words Bahá'u'lláh*. By Bahá'u'lláh
www.bahai.org/r/445619358

Quotation prior to 'Dust', Source: 'Ṭarázát, 1st Taraz, Ornaments,' *Tablets of Baha'u'llah*, by Bahá'u'lláh
www.bahai.org/r/489268445

Quotation prior to 'Hope', Source: *The Poems of Emily Dickinson: Reading Edition*, edited by Ralph W. Franklin, Cambridge, Mass. The Belknap Press of Harvard University Press, Copyright © 1998, 1999 by the President and Fellows of Harvard College. Copyright © 1951, 1955, 1979, 1983 by the President and Fellows of Harvard College.

Quotation prior to 'Listen', Source: *Call of The Divine Beloved*, by Bahá'u'lláh, www.bahai.org/r/580916946

Many thanks to those who have been part of the journey of this book:

Belinda Belton, Michael Day, Heidi Den Ronden, Matilda Elliot, Renee Farrant, Ruha and Minaira Fifita, Jocelyn Hawes, Melanie Hill, Dr Janet Khan, Sheridan Perkins, The Ink of Light Bahá'í Writers Festival, Pixi Robertson, Françoise Teclemariam, James Tichenor, Ayesha Uddin and the Wilmette Institute.

NSA of the Bahá'ís of Australia for Bahá'í Review.

Also, many thanks to Grant Hindin Miller for writing the Foreword.

Foreword

There's a saying on the wall of a monastery on Mt Athos:

Sister Almond tree,
Speak to us of God,
And the Almond tree ... blossomed

This image and saying remind me of the spirit and poetry of June Perkins, whose carefully selected phrases are proffered with open palms; and whose simplicity, beauty, and transcendence, like the Almond blossom, are self-evident.

When June writes:

First light
soft peach spreading over
    earth's green skin

... she is dipping and diving 'into the river of the heart light', and, in relaying 'her own story ...becomes more than body and bones'.

Here we have a respectful, receptive witness: her 'field has dreams' and her senses are open 'to the scent of the divine'. So, when her 'soul catches light' she takes the time to 'tap' on her 'divine keyboard' and helps us all 'escape our day's cage in the bird of poetry'.

I recently met June at a Writer's Festival in Brisbane. If you have the good fortune of meeting this smiling woman you'll experience, immediately, the warmth of a benign and other-worldly presence. You may not know that she has done the hard intellectual yards and attained a PhD (in the empowerment of Indigenous women through writing) or that she has numerous belles lettres to her name. What you will experience is a radiance of spirit and a magnanimous humility.

These qualities rise like swirls and oxygenated bubbles in her lines; they are 'like apprentice oars' that are willing 'to learn the Rhythms of the River'.

Most of us live distracted and demanding lives. We can be grateful that when June Perkins picks up her quill she helps us 'remember the scent of oranges'.

Grant Hindin Miller, September, 2019

June Perkins

Illuminations

The Dreamer

Do you see only
    an empty field
        a harvest been and gone?

Look again
    another planting
        is on its way.

This field has dreams.

Artist's Riddle

It moves a dancer
to the music.

It quickens oil and acrylic
into paintings.

It inspires the weave of a
basket.

It gifts the words
to the writer.

It beams stage light
on the actors' faces.

It follows them
scene by scene.

It calls artist
to their subjects.

It guides them
> to find their calling.

It frees them
> from the dance.

It frees them
> from the paint.

It frees them
> from the words.

It brings the eternal
> brilliance.

It guides them to
> the next worlds' calling.

Boonah Morning

Wells of silence, so quiet
    not even a pin drops.

Boonah morning beckons
    the sunrise mist.

Sunrise spills on the fence lines –
    certitude.

Sunrise melody illumines
    the seeker's face.

The bird on the wire greets
    Boonah, with her songs
        for dreamers.

The Poetry Bird

Maya Angelou tells me why
    the caged bird always sings.

Bahá'u'lláh sings
    the soul a bird,
        the body its cage.

Maya tells me
    I'm a *Phenomenal Woman*.

Bahá'u'lláh says
    'Humanity has two wings:
        man and woman,
        now woman must fly too.'

I escape rhymes
    with no reason.

I escape my day's cage
      in the bird of poetry.

Once a young woman listening to jazz,
      I'm older now
           improvising my journey
      still a lover of Light.

My life's sunset could be in a moment
      or years from now.

Whatever will be
      will be, so long as,
      the soul keeps singing
          its song.

I'm just a bird looking to
      escape my day's cage in
           the bird of poetry.

Poet's Tree

What kind of tree is your
poet's tree?

      Is it a boab, oak
      paperbark or willow?

Does it dance with Mandela
or meditate with Mahatma?

      Is it a haven for
      Maya Angelou's caged birds?

How many poets who
once waged war
created peace odes for
soldiers who lay bloodied and
lost at the base of this tree?

Does your tree sing
walking stick poems
      to heal?

The Nightingale sings
      from the branches
      of my poet's tree
      leads me into the heart
           of things beyond.

What kind of tree is
your poet's tree?

Nine Illuminations

I
A hint of purple
on crossroads of cobblestone
illumination beckons...

II
This boat has a story
carrying humanity's dreams
in a future unseen.

Two oars, still,
waiting for the apprentice
to learn rhythms of the river.

III
'Release me,' sang the soul
as if it were a bird.
Its wings rippling prayers
the Great Spirit heard.

IV
Give me cracks where
art escapes concrete
      to
         blossom
         into songs of
            renewal.

V
Mirage world shimmers
deceiving moments until
prayers bring focus.

VI
Visionary sees
a feather's potential
to be
wing, pen or symbol.

Lost and found
visionary ibis dreams
her feather's journey
in flight.

VII
Everlasting life
      sing me a river
           full of virtues . . .

VIII

Soul ladder made of
      guitar strings
           sending notes to
                  the brilliant stars.

You are a shining lamp
      navigating meaning
           with melody.

IX
Encountering turtles
>trapped in deathly
>ghost nets,

beach combing children remember
>asking father
>endless questions
>beginning with
>>'Why?'

>*Nothing was too much trouble*
>*And there was always time.*

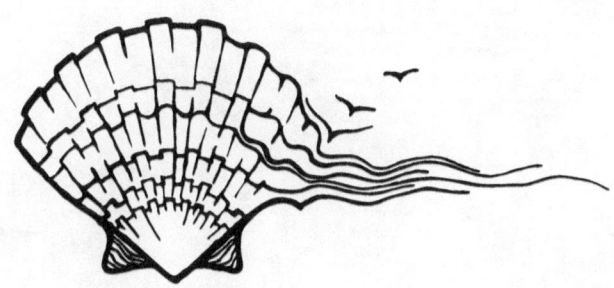

Swirling, Almost Something

For Nance and Ray

An abstract painting, full of swirling almost something shapes, hangs above the stairs in the hall entrance, capturing the attention of every visitor to Nance's.

    All are struck by it, especially children. Nance looks at them warmly and invites analysis: *'What do you think it is?'* She adds their views to those from earlier visitors. She only shares those past interpretations with them after they offer their own.

Nance attends the *University of the Third Age* and is an avid reader who has never stopped questioning and being open to the ways of the world. Nestled in her seaside home she might seem as if she has retreated from most of the world. Certainly, she has carved out a nest of memory and solitude to which others are welcome. Yet, she is still concerned with the world and all the wisdom beyond her retreat. *'What he says makes a lot of sense,'* she is telling the story of some guru in India who she has recently been reading and recommends to us. *'No one has sole tabs on the truth,'* she muses. *'So many pathways lead to the same God.'*

Mementos of overseas travels and teaching sabbaticals with her husband are everywhere. He is gone, yet near in every conversation. He passed away from a heart condition soon after retiring. Yet this is no home of grief, rather one where every memory is treasured and embodied in every object: the intangible, it seems, breathes.

'Yes, that's from when Ray and I were at...'

Nance introduces me to ginger kiss biscuits: her favourite thing to offer visitors, along with raisin toast and some tea.

Now, eating ginger kisses always reminds me of her and brings her advice back as if on fortune cookie paper running a reminder reel in my head.

She offers the sage advice which has kept her in good stead all her life:

'Never go to sleep angry with your partner.'

'If you can afford it get a housekeeper; if you are working, don't try to do it all.'

'Children remember the love – not how good a housekeeper you are.'

She looks after a shack, owned by Quakers, and located right next to her house. It's low cost accommodation for people wanting to temporarily escape the stresses of city life. Its owners are happy for her to book in Bahá'í friends whenever needed.

A visitor's book inside the shack is full of comments, such as: 'We enjoyed our freedom from television and other distractions.'
'We love that there are fishing rods, board games and we're a short walk to the beach.'

We stay next to Nance, in our own family space. A few times we pop over for afternoon tea and a chat during our times by the sea.

Later, whilst I am writing up my PhD, we live around the corner from Nance for a year. It is then I notice, Nance drives friends with cancer to hospital. She picks up people without transport to bring them to meetings. She visits those who cannot go out easily.

Nance's house is neat, tidy and a row of cyclamens dresses the windowsill. She can look out on the ocean from her front veranda.

Her children and grandchildren visit now and then. Her daughter's family eventually live in the house, downstairs.

Nance shapes how I see:
…time
…true love
…memory.

These things are embodied in ginger kiss biscuits; questions concerning the intangible; and her sage advice, returning when I need it most.
    Nance will forever be in the painting, full of swirling, almost something.

I am the Mystic Fane which the Hand of Omnipotence hath reared. I am the Lamp which the Finger of God hath lit within its niche and caused to shine with deathless splendour. I am the Flame of that supernal Light that glowed upon Sinai in the gladsome Spot, and lay concealed in the midst of the Burning Bush.

The Báb

Declaration

For Mullá Husayn

First realisation
> does not rush into the open.

It is hampered by the doubts
> of the listener.

He wants proof
> to unlock the Gate.

It arrives unasked for
> Surih of Joseph then

First realisation:
> now he is
>> the gate to the Gate.

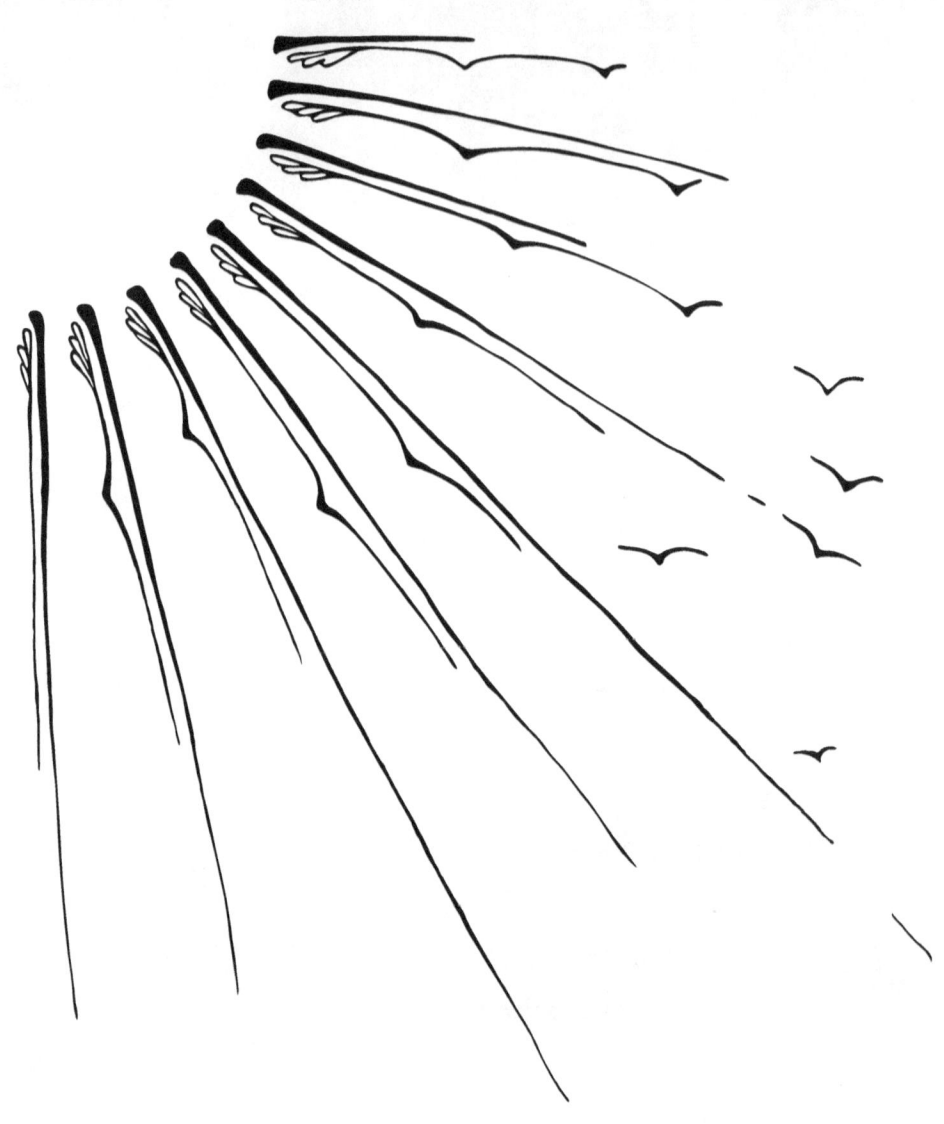

First Light

First light
soft peach spreading over
    earth's green skin.

Its glimmerings
    promise warmth to bathe in.

Monochromes of green
    spilling then
    dancing
    everywhere.

New ways spreading seeds,
    planting them soul by soul.

Souls catching light
    drinking it in
    breathing it out because
    Mullá Husayn has woken
        to taste the first light.

Dawn Breakers

Waking in the emerging rose lit dawn,
      one by one colours emerge
           from pale grey.

Stirring whisperings
      of the Mystic Fane
           rising note by note.

Barely spoken colours
      could not resist moving
           towards beginnings.

Something bringing
      safety disguised as danger
           crept around them.

They thought they dreamt
      though they were waking.

A swirling wind mover
      blew them forward
           to the Fort of Fate,
        Ṭabarsí.

Sacrifices to the dawn
      the reverberations of their shouts
     caressing indigo as lovers
        waking to the crown
          of martyrdom.

In Faith

For Táhirih

Be a hollow reed
      welcoming melodies
      with notes breathing skies
and skies breathing blue
      and blue breathing sea
and sea breathing woman.

A woman breathing
      your unveiling and
        peeling away
      the skin of your ego
loosening and falling
      a cocoon disappearing

In Badasht last century
          the morn.

The Green Broom

Voice of the Báb's Servant Mubarak

Sweeping,
    sweeping pathways
        to make a befitting place
        for Him
        to walk with Khadijih.

Sweeping,
    sweeping the autumn leaves
        falling,
        falling.

    Still not here.

Watching winter trees
        turn into pencil grey outlines
            nothing to sweep.

Assuring her, with certitude
        'He will return.'

Waiting, waiting ...

Whither can a lover go but to the land of his beloved?
Bahá'u'lláh

Prince of Peace

There He is.
I can't see His smile
just a hint of His hand
from a window.

I have travelled so far to
see Him.
I am so near
I could run up the stairs
to kneel humbly at His feet
however, the door is closed.

Every day outside Akka
I stand on the corner thinking,
There He is.

I feel His smile
transforming
the pith of me.

The rumour of His life
and words have moved me
to journey here.

I am not disappointed
for His kindness falls
from that window.
Its presence
in every leaf falling.

His purity is
no rumour.
His breath
is clearing the city's
pollution, sorrow, and disunity.

His footsteps
are gentle to the earth.
Yet He is not abased,
this pure mirror,
reflecting glories
one can only long to
see the silhouettes of.

He is truly here.
This Promised One
Fifth Buddha
Manifestation of the Lord of Hosts
Prince of Peace.

His gaze touches
each tree
each person waiting
all the shadows too.

I remember the scent of
oranges
now reminding me I must
make
the long journey, home.

I rejoice for I was so near.
I offered prayers for His
safety
for the glory of His mission
for other seekers to
find nearness.

Unwillingly
I will take my feet away
and leave with
my life forever dedicated.

No city can contain Him,
nor prison detain Him.
Yet remoteness from Him
is unbearable.

Even though I only saw His hand
wisdom wafts
in every pocket of air
around me now.

When I leave
I will carry it on my sleeves
in my hair
within my heart
and whisper it to you.

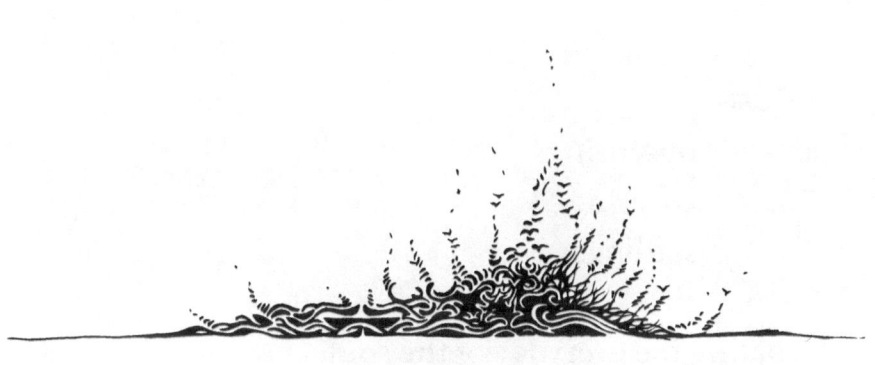

We cherish the hope that through the loving-kindness of the All-Wise, the All-Knowing, obscuring dust may be dispelled, and the power of perception enhanced, that the people may discover the purpose for which they have been called into being.

Bahá'u'lláh

Dust

Dust
    obscuring
    covering
    settling

coating the everyday of the soul.

    A thickening mantle of swirling

    loss
    regret
    anxiety
    confusion

        self-doubt
        surrounds
        impounds
        confounds.

Questions asked of a higher power
        astound.

The shape of the spirit unfurls
　　　tips of wings
　　　for a moment visible . . .
　　　　　　　　faith
　　　　　　　　connection
　　　　　　　　certainty.

Divine breeze released by words
　　　chanted
　　　recited
　　　carried by the air
　　　　　　through
　　　melody, free from dust.

Then an air filter sounds a warning
　　　　　the arrival of more dust.

Slipstream

Slipstream,
> I look for you
>> somewhere in the
>>> memoryland
>>>> homeland
>>>>> heartstream.

I fly in you and sigh in you.

Memoryland
> when I understand you
>> you gift me
>> wisdom plumes.

Yet am I covered and ready for flight?

Homeland,
> are you in motherland, fatherland
>> or all the spaces I connect with?

Soaring to understand
> homeland, memoryland,
>> cyclone's hands…

Can I move forward
> to global skies
>> beyond histories' lies
> to find – why I try to glide?

My heartland
> my strength
> grows in
> the wounds of
>> the slipstream.

Elixir

Elixir string
holds my soul ring
makes a coat of blue tones
pares music back to its bones.

My blue note
bends in the moonlight
dips and dives
in the river of
the heart light.

While shimmers
on the Artist's lake
say, 'Let my soul wake.'

Word Fragrance

His Word animates my hands
    to tap out reminders of
        divine fragrance in
            everyday experiences
    And see the rapture
        in the ordinary.

Sometimes in the morning
    a divine muse
        brings these thoughts:

'My body and culture
    are garments from which my soul
        seeks release
    to sense its own fragrance
        to dance its own dance
        to tell its own story
        become more than
            body and bones.'

Limited by the world I can see
      curious about the world I cannot
      I wonder if in the next world
      this story will be
      tapped on a divine keyboard

              or etched in ink.

Dear Artist

Improvise your beauty
    from life's wisdom.

Syncopate your melody
    to the scent of the divine.

Worship with soaring notes
    the Holy Spirit.

Elevate your rapture
    to the metaphors nature provides.

Avoid the boxes of slim definitions,
    ego and fear.

Educate, ennoble and enchant with
    divine beauty
    so hard to explain
        yet easy to recognize when
        expressed and given as a gift.

Experiment in meditation
      paint the everyday
      into a rose.

Pluck thorns of inertia
      from the vocabulary of your being.

Imagine virtue as a brush.

Be more than your body
      more than your bones
           more than your voice.

Now, can you hear the muse
      sing within you?

"Hope" is the thing with feathers –
That perches in the soul –
And sings the tune without the words –
And never stops – at all –

Emily Dickinson

Hope

A thing with feathers
        perhaps a kingfisher
        small and blue
perches on a branch of
        a gum tree in my backyard
        and starts to sing.

Does it chirp?
        Does it twitter?
        I must confess I have not listened.
            Perhaps hope is like that.

And yet
        it keeps on wanting to be
            noticed, however diffident
                    its song.

When encouraged
    it swoops down
        scoops up some soul in
flight.

    Or is hope like Pandora's box
        which when opened
            overwhelms and teases
        the poet
            curious to write

                I hope?

O My friend, listen with heart and soul to the songs of the spirit, and treasure them as thine own eyes.

Baháʼuʼlláh

Listen

I'm searching for songs of the spirit
passing wisdom onto me,
and seeking within their tunes
virtues to set me free.

Escaping spaces too earthly
meditating on spheres unseen,
I turn my mirror to heaven
for strength to wipe it clean.

Listening with heart and soul
my essence begins to unfold,
as I hear the songs of the spirit
in a symphony to behold.

Notes to the Poems

THE ARTIST'S RIDDLE

The answer to the riddle is the Holy Spirit;

which, through the mediation of the Prophets of God, teaches spiritual virtues to man and enables him to attain Eternal Life. All these blessings are brought to man by the Holy Spirit; therefore, we can understand that the Holy Spirit is the Intermediary between the Creator and the created. The light and heat of the sun cause the earth to be fruitful and create life in all things that grow; and the Holy Spirit quickens the souls of men.

'Abdu'l-Bahá *Paris Talks*, p. 58.

BOONAH MORNING

Boonah is a town in Queensland, about an hour's drive from Brisbane.

THE POETRY BIRD

Maya Angelou (1928-2014) was an American poet, memoirist, and civil rights activist. She published seven autobiographies, three books of essays, several books of poetry. I refer to her poems 'Caged Bird' and 'Phenomenal Women' in this poem.

Bahá'u'lláh, meaning the 'Glory of God', is the founder of the Bahá'í Faith. Born Mirza Husayn-'Alí in Tehran, Iran on 12 November 1817.

Bahá'ís are also referred to as followers of the Light.

POET'S TREE

This poem is playing with the idea of many poets having a tree that they might relate to as a central motif in their work or philosophy, with a pun on poet tree, poetry.

Nelson Mandela (18 July 1918 – 5 December 2013) was a South African anti-apartheid revolutionary, politician, and philanthropist, who served as President of South Africa from 1994 to 1999.

Mahatma Gandhi (1869-1948) was the leader of India's non-violent independence movement against British rule. He advocated for the civil rights of Indians in both South Africa and India. Born in Porbandar, India, Gandhi studied law and organised boycotts against British institutions in peaceful forms of civil disobedience. He was killed by a fanatic in 1948.

Stanza 5 refers to both the First World War Poets and peace poetry and songs of contemporary times.

The metaphor of the *Nightingale* is often used to refer to Bahá'u'lláh (see also 'Prince of Peace').

NINE ILLUMINATIONS

Illumination viii

'where there is love nothing is too much trouble and there is always time,' saying attributed to 'Abdu'l-Bahá (son of Bahá'u'lláh) in *Pilgrim's Notes*. Quoted in *Portals to Freedom* by Howard Colby Ives. I have paraphrased it here and am referencing 'Abdu'l-Bahá's patience to listen to questions.

SWIRLING, ALMOST SOMETHING

Quakers are part of an historically Christian group of religious movements known as the Society of Friends. They believe people should follow their 'inner light' and that God will always guide His creation and over time change the laws.

University of the Third Age, U3A is a self-help organisation promoting learning for personal development and well-being. The three ages being youth, work/homemaking and retirement. It promotes doing interesting new things and making new friends. There are no academic requirements for membership and no exams.

DECLARATION

The Báb (1819-1850) literally 'the Gate'– title of Siyyid Ali-Muhammad, the prophet and founder of the Bábí Faith and the forerunner and herald of Bahá'u'lláh.

Mullá Husayn (1813–1849) also known by the honorific Jináb-i Bábu'l-Báb ("Gate of the Gate"). He was a religious figure in 19th century Persia and the first to recognise the Báb. This poem is inspired by what happened when he met the Báb.

Surih (Sura and Surah) of Joseph – A chapter from the Qur'an, telling the story of Joseph. Joseph's story of peace and forgiveness is also found in the Hebrew Bible, and the Bahá'í writings. The Báb made His claim to Prophethood with His commentary on the Surih of Joseph on the night of His declaration.

The Mystic Fane is one of the names the Báb calls himself.

DAWN BREAKERS

Dawn Breakers is the title of Nabíl's narrative of the early days of the Bahá'í Revelation. He collected testimonies of the early believers to tell the stories of Táhirih, Mullá Husayn, the Báb and more.

'Fort of Fate' refers to Ṭabarsí, a siege between the forces of the Shah of Persia and the Bábís over the period 10 October 1848 to 10 May 1849, when the King resorted to a plan of betrayal to capture the remaining Bábís. The siege was located in the shrine of Shaykh Tabarsi, a twelfth century Persian scholar.

IN FAITH

Táhirih (1814 -1852), a renowned Bábí poet, was probably best remembered for unveiling herself in an assemblage of men during the Conference of Badasht, as a symbol of the new religion's break from Islam. The unveiling caused a great deal of controversy and the Báb named her Táhirih (meaning 'the Pure One') to show his support for her. She was soon placed under house arrest in Tehran. In mid-1852 she was executed in secret due to her Bábí Faith.

The Conference of Badasht was a significant event in Bahá'í history which marked the new religion and was going to revolutionise social laws.

THE GREEN BROOM

This poem is as if spoken by *Mubarak*, an Ethiopian servant of the Báb. No one had the heart to tell him the Báb had been killed by a firing squad for His teachings, fearing the news would break Mubarak's heart.

Khadijih is the wife of the Báb.

PRINCE OF PEACE

This poem is set in the time when Bahá'u'lláh was exiled and imprisoned in Akka and pilgrims were prevented from visiting. Prince of Peace refers to Bahá'u'lláh.

Akka is a city in the Ottoman Empire.

Bahá'u'lláh says He is the fulfilment of many religions, and the Promised one who will bring about the unification of all humanity, in an era called the 'Most Great Peace'. For more on this read the *Kitáb-i-qán*. Some of His names are **Lord of Hosts**, and the Fifth Buddha.

The term "Lord of Hosts" is used in the Bahá'í Faith as a title of God. Bahá'u'lláh, claiming to be a Manifestation of God, wrote tablets to many of the kings and rulers of the world inviting them to recognize Him as the Promised One of all ages and faiths, some of which were compiled and published in English as *The Summons of the Lord of Hosts*.

ELIXIR

Elixir Strings are the #1 selling acoustic guitar strings. They retain their tone longer than any other string, uncoated or coated, according to players.

HOPE

References Emily Dickinson's Poem 314, 'Hope is the thing with Feathers'. See Acknowledgements.

Biographies

AUTHOR

June Perkins is a multi-arts creative born to a Papua New Guinean Indigenous mother and Australian father. She was raised in Tasmania as a Bahá'í and combines poetry, blogging, photography, story and more to explore themes interesting her – peace, ecology, spirituality, cultural diversity, resilience and empowerment. June is currently involved in organising the Ink of Light, Bahá'í Writers Festival.

www.juneperk.wixsite.com/gumbootspearlz

OTHER POETRY PUBLICATIONS

Magic Fish Dreaming (2016)

June has had poems appear in *Nineteen Months*, Queensland Art Gallery (2018), *Illumine* (2017), *Tokens* issue 7-9 (2018-19), the *Australian Children's Poetry* website (2017-2020), *Creative Kids Tales Story Collection 2* (2019), *Spooktacular Stories* (2019), *After Yasi Finding the Smile Within* (2013), *Voices in the North* (2013), *True Spirit of Cyclone Yasi* (2012), *Under One Sky* (2010), *Cracks in the Canopy* (2010), *Etchings 2 and 10* (2007 and 2011), *World Order* Vol 38 1 (2006) on her blogs, and more …

ILLUSTRATORS

Ruha Fifita was born in Vava'u, Tonga and spent most of her life immersed in the culture and vibrancy of life in the Pacific. Her love for visual and performative forms of expression have been nurtured through the support and encouragement of her extended family and study of the writings of the Bahá'í Faith.

Minaira Fifita is a visual and performing artist whose work aspires to reflect her love of creation and faith in the unity of humanity. Her style of creativity blends together her Polynesian and Celtic roots and experiences of vibrancy, balance and harmony within the Pacific and her spiritual beliefs as a Bahá'í.

For more on their work: @ivi-designs

From the Readers

I was curious about the language of adoration, worship, and rapture you use in the more spiritual poems. The commonality amongst believers, regardless of faith, binds us. We recognise the same experience of faith in each other, and I think that is cause for celebration.

    Melanie Hill, Poet

Very deeply felt and flowing verse, reminding me of thought patterns in the Eastern spiritual tradition. 'The Poetry Bird', 'Swirling, Almost Something', 'Prince of Peace' and 'The Dreamer' each struck a chord in me, seeming particularly gentle and transcendent.

    Ayesha Uddin, Librettist, Engineer, and Writer

I enjoyed the stream of consciousness. Some of the poems reminded me of Rabindranath Tagore's work.

    Jocelyn Hawes, Children's Author and Christian.

'Artist's Riddle' strongly resonates with me so I have stuck a copy on my office wall. Like 'Word Fragrance' and 'Dear Artist', it points to the mysterious wafting of inspiration from the spiritual realms. *Illuminations* is a blessed gift from the poet. Produced at a precious time, the Bicentenary of the Birth of the Báb.

    Michael Day, Bahá'í Author

www.ingramcontent.com/pod-product-compliance
Lightning Source LLC
Chambersburg PA
CBHW030448300426
44112CB00009B/1222